E.P.L.

S0-EAV-625

A Beginning-to-Read Book

PHYSICAL SCIENCE

SPEED

by Mary Lindeen

NORWOOD HOUSE PRESS

DEAR CAREGIVER, The *Beginning to Read—Read and Discover Science* books provide young readers the opportunity to learn about scientific concepts while simultaneously building early reading skills. Each title corresponds to three of the key domains within the Next Generation Science Standards (NGSS): physical sciences, life sciences, and earth and space sciences.

The NGSS include standards that are comprised of three dimensions: Cross-cutting Concepts, Science and Engineering Practices, and Disciplinary Core Ideas. The texts within the *Read and Discover Science* series focus primarily upon the Disciplinary Core Ideas and Cross-cutting Concepts—helping readers view their world through a scientific lens. They pique a young reader's curiosity and encourage them to inquire and explore. The Connecting Concepts section at the back of each book offers resources to continue that exploration. The reinforcement activities at the back of the book support Science and Engineering Practices—to understand how scientists investigate phenomena in that world.

These easy-to-read informational texts make the scientific concepts accessible to young readers and prompt them to consider the role of science in their world. On one hand, these titles can develop background knowledge for exploring new topics. Alternately, they can be used to investigate, explain, and expand the findings of one's own inquiry. As you read with your child, encourage her or him to "observe"—taking notice of the images and information to formulate both questions and responses about what, how, and why something is happening.

Above all, the most important part of the reading experience is to have fun and enjoy it!

Sincerely,

Shannon Cannon

Shannon Cannon, Ph.D.
Literacy Consultant

Norwood House Press • P.O. Box 316598 • Chicago, Illinois 60631
For more information about Norwood House Press please visit our website at
www.norwoodhousepress.com or call 866-565-2900.
© 2018 Norwood House Press. Beginning-to-Read™ is a trademark of Norwood House Press.
All rights reserved. No part of this book may be reproduced or utilized in any form or by any
means without written permission from the publisher.

Editor: Judy Kentor Schmauss
Designer: Lindaanne Donohoe

Photo Credits:

Shutterstock: cover, 1, 3, 8-9, 10-11, 12-13, 14-15, 18-19, 20-21, 22-23
iStock: 4-5, 6-7, 16-17, 24-25, 26-27

Library of Congress Cataloging-in-Publication Data
Names: Lindeen, Mary, author.
Title: Speed / by Mary Lindeen.
Description: Chicago, Illinois : Norwood House Press, 2017 | Series: A
beginning-to-read book | Audience: K to 3.
Identifiers: LCCN 2017002629 (print) | LCCN 2017008553 (ebook) | ISBN
9781599538808 (library edition ; alk. paper) | ISBN 9781684041121 (eBook)
Subjects: LCSH: Speed—Juvenile literature. | Force and energy—Juvenile
literature.
Classification: LCC QC137.52 .L56 2017 (print) | LCC QC137.52 (ebook) | DDC
531/.112—dc23
LC record available at https://lccn.loc.gov/2017002629

Library ISBN: 978-1-59953-880-8   Paperback ISBN: 978-1-68404-099-5

302N—072017
Manufactured in the United States of America in North Mankato, Minnesota.

A soccer ball sits in the grass.
It doesn't move.

If you kick the ball, it speeds through the air!

Your foot pushes the ball into motion.

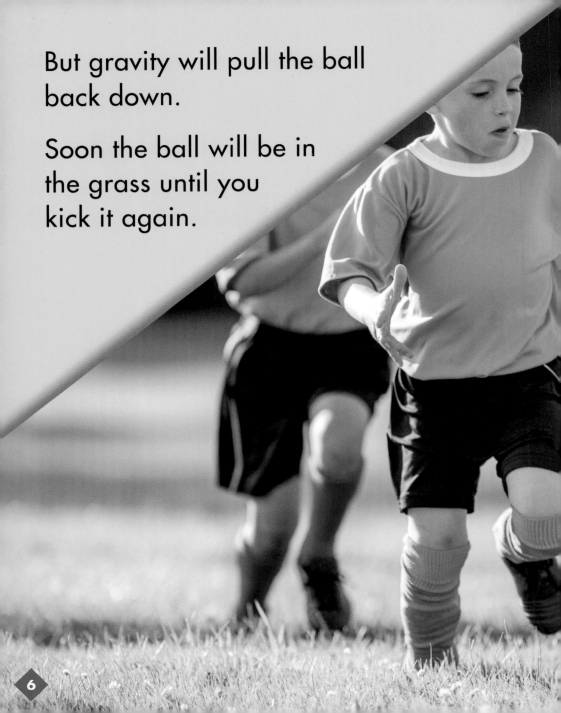

But gravity will pull the ball
back down.

Soon the ball will be in
the grass until you
kick it again.

Did You Know?

We can't see forces, but we can see how they affect objects.

Pushes and pulls are forces.

Forces can make
objects move.

Forces can make objects move fast.

The harder you kick a ball, the faster the ball moves.

Did You Know?

A scientist who studies speed and motion is called a physicist.

The harder you pull a wagon,
the faster the wagon goes.

The harder you push on
the pedals of your bike,
the faster it goes.

The harder you pull on a zipper, the faster it goes up and down.

Forces can slow the speed of an object, too.

Air pushing on the inside of a parachute slows its fall.

Pulling on your dog's leash slows it from a run to a walk.

bike brake
pushing on tire

Forces can make objects stop, too.

The brakes on your bike
push against the wheels
to make them
stop turning.

You push your skates against the ice when you want to stop.

You pull on a spring
to stop it from
snapping back
into place.

Pushes and pulls make objects stop and go.
They speed things up and slow them down.
The forces of motion are always at work!

Push

Pull

CONNECTING CONCEPTS

UNDERSTANDING SCIENCE CONCEPTS

To check your child's understanding of the information in this book, recreate the following graphic organizer on a sheet of paper. Help your child complete the organizer by comparing the forces of push and pull:

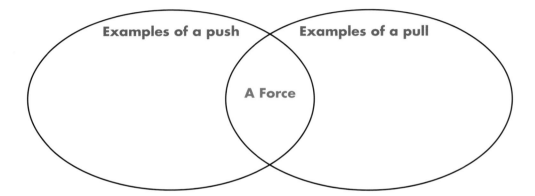

Examples of a push   Examples of a pull

A Force

SCIENCE IN THE REAL WORLD

With your child, make a list of things each of you does in a normal day. Include even the most minor activities. Write them down and then decide if any of the activities involved the force of pushing or pulling and if so, how.

SCIENCE AND ACADEMIC LANGUAGE

Make sure your child understands the meaning of the following words:

pushes   motion   gravity   pull   forces   objects   scientist   physicist   speed

Have him or her use the words in a sentence.

FLUENCY

Help your child practice fluency by using one or more of the following activities:

1. Reread the book to your child at least two times while he or she uses a finger to track each word as it is read.

2. Read a line of the book, then reread it as your child reads along with you.

3. Ask your child to go back through the book and read the words he or she knows.

4. Have your child practice reading the book several times to improve accuracy, rate, and expression.

FOR FURTHER INFORMATION

Books:

Minden, Cecilia. *Push and Pulls*. Ann Arbor, MI: Cherry Lake, 2016.

Sohn, Emily. *Experiments in Forces and Motion with Toys and Everyday Stuff*. Mankato, MN: Capstone, 2015.

Weakland, Mark. *Thud!: Wile E. Coyote Experiments with Forces and Motion*. Mankato, MN: Capstone Press, 2014.

Websites:

Idaho Public Television: Force and Motion Facts

http://idahoptv.org/sciencetrek/topics/force_and_motion/facts.cfm

BBC School: Pushes and Pulls

http://www.bbc.co.uk/schools/scienceclips/ages/5_6/pushes_pulls.shtml

STEM from the Start: Motion (Parts 1 and 2)

http://video.nhptv.org/show/stem-start/

Word List

Speed uses the 90 words listed below. *High-frequency* words are those words that are used most often in the English language. They are sometimes referred to as sight words because children need to learn to recognize them automatically when they read. *Content words* are any words specific to a particular topic. Regular practice reading these words will enhance your child's ability to read with greater fluency and comprehension.

High-Frequency Words

a	at	from	it	see	too	will
again	back	go	its	the	until	work
air	be	how	make	them	up	you
always	but	if	of	they	want	your
an	called	in	on	things	we	
and	can	into	place	through	when	
are	down	is	run	to	who	

Content Words

affect	dog's	gravity	move(s)	scientist	speed(s)	wheels
against	fall	harder	object(s)	sits	spring	zipper
ball	fast(er)	ice	parachute	skates	stop	
bike	foot	inside	pedals	slow(s)	studies	
brakes	forces	kick	physicist	snapping	turning	
can't	goes	leash	pull(s, ing)	soccer	wagon	
doesn't	grass	motion	push(es, ing)	soon	walk	

About the Author

Mary Lindeen is a writer, editor, parent, and former elementary school teacher. She has written more than 100 books for children and edited many more. She specializes in early literacy instruction and books for young readers, especially nonfiction.

About the Advisor

Dr. Shannon Cannon is an elementary school teacher in Sacramento, California. She has served as a teacher educator in the School of Education at UC Davis, where she also earned her Ph.D. in Language, Literacy, and Culture. As a member of the clinical faculty, she supervised pre-service teachers and taught elementary methods courses in reading, effective teaching, and teacher action research.